PREPARATORY SET #2

RUDIMENTS EXAM SERIES ANSWERS

By Glory St. Germain ARCT RMT MYCC UMTC
Shelagh McKibbon-U'Ren RMT UMTC

ULTIMATE MUSIC THEORY

GSG MUSIC

Enriching Lives Through Music Education

ISBN: 978-1-927641-09-5

The Ultimate Music Theory™ Program
Enriching Lives Through Music Education

The Ultimate Music Theory™ Workbooks & Answer Books Program includes:

UMT Rudiments Workbooks for Prep 1, Prep 2, Basic, Intermediate, Advanced & Complete
UMT Exam Series (Set #1 & Set #2) for Preparatory, Basic, Intermediate & Advanced

Supplemental Workbooks for PREP LEVEL, LEVELS 1 - 8 & COMPLETE LEVEL
UMT Supplemental Exam Series for LEVEL 5, LEVEL 6, LEVEL 7 & LEVEL 8

The Ultimate Music Theory Program is the *Way to Score Success* as UMT helps students prepare for nationally recognized theory examinations including the Royal Conservatory of Music.

 Library and Archives Canada Cataloguing in Publication. UMT Workbooks & Exam Series /Glory St. Germain & Shelagh McKibbon-U'Ren. Respect Copyright. All rights reserved. GlorylandPublishing.com

Ultimate Music Theory Rudiments Exam Series

GP - EPS1	ISBN: 978-1-927641-00-2	Preparatory Rudiments Exams Set #1
GP - EPS1A	ISBN: 978-1-927641-08-8	Preparatory Exams Answers Set #1
GP - EPS2	ISBN: 978-1-927641-01-9	Preparatory Rudiments Exams Set #2
GP - EPS2A	ISBN: 978-1-927641-09-5	Preparatory Exams Answers Set #2
GP - EBS1	ISBN: 978-1-927641-02-6	Basic Rudiments Exams Set #1
GP - EBS1A	ISBN: 978-1-927641-10-1	Basic Exams Answers Set #1
GP - EBS2	ISBN: 978-1-927641-03-3	Basic Rudiments Exams Set #2
GP - EBS2A	ISBN: 978-1-927641-11-8	Basic Exams Answers Set #2
GP - EIS1	ISBN: 978-1-927641-04-0	Intermediate Rudiments Exams Set #1
GP - EIS1A	ISBN: 978-1-927641-12-5	Intermediate Exams Answers Set #1
GP - EIS2	ISBN: 978-1-927641-05-7	Intermediate Rudiments Exams Set #2
GP - EIS2A	ISBN: 978-1-927641-13-2	Intermediate Exams Answers Set #2
GP - EAS1	ISBN: 978-1-927641-06-4	Advanced Rudiments Exams Set #1
GP - EAS1A	ISBN: 978-1-927641-14-9	Advanced Exams Answers Set #1
GP - EAS2	ISBN: 978-1-927641-07-1	Advanced Rudiments Exams Set #2
GP - EAS2A	ISBN: 978-1-927641-15-6	Advanced Exams Answers Set #2

Ultimate Music Theory Supplemental Exam Series

GP-L5E	ISBN: 978-1-990358-11-1	LEVEL 5 Exams
GP-L5EA	ISBN: 978-1-990358-12-8	LEVEL 5 Exams Answers
GP-L6E	ISBN: 978-1-990358-13-5	LEVEL 6 Exams
GP-L6EA	ISBN: 978-1-990358-14-2	LEVEL 6 Exams Answers
GP-L7E	ISBN: 978-1-990358-15-9	LEVEL 7 Exams
GP-L7EA	ISBN: 978-1-990358-16-6	LEVEL 7 Exams Answers
GP-L8E	ISBN: 978-1-990358-17-3	LEVEL 8 Exams
GP-L8EA	ISBN: 978-1-990358-18-0	LEVEL 8 Exams Answers

Go to UltimateMusicTheory.com and check out the FREE Resources

Ultimate Music Theory FREE RESOURCES created just for you!

The **Ultimate Music Theory Exams** reinforce the **UMT Prep 1 and Prep 2 Rudiments Workbooks** and prepare students for continued learning with UMT Basic Rudiments.

Preparatory Rudiments Theory Examination requirements are:

Pitch
- Grand Staff (Treble Clef or G Clef and Bass Clef or F Clef)
- Note names (up to two ledger lines below and above the Treble Clef and Bass Clef)
- Accidentals (sharp, flat and natural signs)
- Whole tones (whole steps) and semitones (half steps)
- Matching notes to the corresponding keys on the keyboard
- Naming or drawing notes on the staff that are shown on a keyboard

Rhythm
- Note and rest time values (whole, half, quarter and eighth)
- Dotted half notes and dotted quarter notes
- Adding Time Signatures, bar lines and rests to a given line of music
- Simple Time Signatures ($\frac{2}{4}$, $\frac{3}{4}$, $\frac{4}{4}$, and $\mathbf{C}$)

Scales in the keys of C Major, G Major and F Major
- Write or identify: Scales, ascending or descending, one octave
- Key Signatures
- Tonic scale degree

Triads in the keys of C Major, G Major and F Major
- Write or identify: Solid (blocked) in Root Position, beginning on the Tonic note (with or without a Key Signature)
- Identify: Broken in Root Position, beginning on the Tonic note (with or without a Key Signature)

Intervals
- Write or identify: above a given note, all intervals up to and including an octave (numerical size only), melodic or harmonic
- Identify: below a given note, all intervals up to and including an octave (numerical size only), melodic form only

Musical Terms and Signs
- Recognize, define or supply the musical terms or signs as listed in the Prep 1 and Prep 2 Ultimate Music Theory Workbooks

Analysis
- Analyze a short musical composition, identifying any of the above theory requirements

Score:
  60 - 69 Pass; **70 - 79** Honors; **80 - 89** First Class Honors; **90 - 100** First Class Honors with Distinction

Ultimate Music Theory: *The Way to Score Success!*

UltimateMusicTheory.com © Copyright 2013 Gloryland Publishing. All Rights Reserved.

… **ULTIMATE MUSIC THEORY**
PREPARATORY EXAM SET #2 - EXAM #1

Total Score: ___
100

> ♪ **UMT Tip:** Middle C can be written in the Treble Clef or in the Bass Clef. Notes above (to the right on the keyboard) of Middle C will be written in the Treble Clef. Notes below (to the left on the keyboard) of Middle C will be written in the Bass Clef.

1. a) Write the notes on the Grand Staff for the keys marked with a ☺. Use whole notes.
   b) Name the notes.
   c) Draw a line from each note to the corresponding key on the keyboard (at the correct pitch).

   10

F   C   G   A   D   A

> ♪ **UMT Tip:** A Key Signature affects all the notes on the staff (and on ledger lines) with the same letter name.

1. d) Name the following notes. (Observe the Key Signature.)

D   E   B♭   B♭   C   E

UltimateMusicTheory.com © Copyright 2013 Gloryland Publishing. All Rights Reserved.

ULTIMATE MUSIC THEORY
PREPARATORY EXAM SET #2 - EXAM #1

♪ **UMT Tip:** When writing the note one semitone above a given note using the same letter name, accidentals will be used to raise the given note.

2. a) Write the note that is one semitone above each of the given notes. Use the same letter name. Use whole notes. Name both notes.

10

♪ **UMT Tip:** When writing the note one semitone below a given note using the same letter name, accidentals will be used to lower the given note.

b) Write the note that is one semitone below each of the given notes. Use the same letter name. Use whole notes. Name both notes.

UltimateMusicTheory.com © Copyright 2013 Gloryland Publishing. All Rights Reserved.

ULTIMATE MUSIC THEORY
PREPARATORY EXAM SET #2 - EXAM #1

> ♪ **UMT Tip:** When naming the interval (number size only), always count from the bottom (lower) note to the top (higher) note. Accidentals do not affect the number size of the interval.

3. Name each of the following intervals. (Write the number size only.)

> ♪ **UMT Tip:** When writing the note a whole tone (whole step) above a note, use neighbouring (next-door) letter names. Write the notes separately (one note after the other). Draw a small keyboard to help you find the correct notes.

4. Write the note that is a whole tone above each given note. Use whole notes.

ULTIMATE MUSIC THEORY
PREPARATORY EXAM SET #2 - EXAM #1

> ♪ **UMT Tip:** When writing a scale going up or down one octave, the Tonic note is the first note and the last (final) note. The Roman Numeral "**I**" is used to label the Tonic note.

5. a) Write the scale of F Major, descending (going down) one octave. Use accidentals instead of a Key Signature. Use whole notes. Circle two Tonic notes. Label them **I**.

b) Write the scale of G Major, ascending (going up) one octave. Use accidentals instead of a Key Signature. Use whole notes. Circle two Tonic notes. Label them **I**.

c) Add a Treble Clef or a Bass Clef at the beginning of the following staff to form the C Major Scale (ascending).

d) Write the Key Signature and the Tonic note for each of the following keys. Use whole notes.

ULTIMATE MUSIC THEORY
PREPARATORY EXAM SET #2 - EXAM #1

> ♪ **UMT Tip:** A solid (blocked) triad is written one note above the other (together; all 3 notes on lines or all 3 notes in spaces). The root note is the bottom (lowest) note.
> A broken triad is written one note after the other (separately; all 3 notes on lines or all 3 notes in spaces). The root note is the bottom (lowest) note.

6. a) Identify the root note of each triad.
   b) Circle whether the triad is Solid or Broken.

[10]

a) Root: __C__   Root: __G__   Root: __F__

b) Solid   (Solid)   Solid
   (Broken)   Broken   (Broken)

a) Root: __G__   Root: __F__   Root: __G__

b) (Solid)   Solid   (Solid)
   Broken   (Broken)   Broken

a) Root: __C__   Root: __G__   Root: __F__   Root: __F__

b) (Solid)   (Solid)   (Solid)   (Solid)
   Broken   Broken   Broken   Broken

ULTIMATE MUSIC THEORY
PREPARATORY EXAM SET #2 - EXAM #1

> ♪ **UMT Tip:** In 4/4 time, a quarter note equals one count.

7. a) Name the type of rests. Indicate the number of counts each rest receives in 4/4 time.

Rest:	whole	half	quarter	eighth
Count:	4	2	1	½

b) Name the type of notes. Indicate the number of counts each note receives in 4/4 time.

Note:	dotted half	half	eighth
Count:	3	2	½

Note:	whole	dotted quarter	2 eighths
Count:	4	1½	1

ULTIMATE MUSIC THEORY
PREPARATORY EXAM SET #2 - EXAM #1

> ♪ UMT Tip: 𝄴 is known as Common Time. It is the same as 4/4.

8. a) Add bar lines to complete the following rhythms.

> ♪ UMT Tip: A whole rest is used for a whole measure of silence.

b) Add rests below each bracket to complete each measure.

UltimateMusicTheory.com © Copyright 2013 Gloryland Publishing. All Rights Reserved.

ULTIMATE MUSIC THEORY
PREPARATORY EXAM SET #2 - EXAM #1

> ♪ **UMT Tip:** Before looking at the possible definitions, look at the Term and identify the definition. Then match the definition with one of the given definitions.

9. Match each musical term with its English definition. (Not all definitions will be used.)

___/10

Term		Definition
a tempo	e	a) very slow
legato	g	b) fast
staccato	i	c) at a moderate tempo
ritardando, rit.	h	d) cancels a sharp or a flat
allegro	b	e) return to the original tempo
diminuendo, dim.	j	f) moderately slow; at a walking pace
largo	a	g) smooth
crescendo, cresc.	k	h) slowing down gradually
moderato	c	i) detached
andante	f	j) becoming softer
		k) becoming louder

ULTIMATE MUSIC THEORY
PREPARATORY EXAM SET #2 - EXAM #1

> ♪ **UMT Tip:** The root of a triad is the lower (bottom) note of the triad.

10. Analyze the following excerpt of music by answering the questions below.

Minuet and Trio

Andante — Ludwig van Beethoven

a) Name the title of this excerpt. __Minuet and Trio__

b) Name the composer of this excerpt. __Ludwig van Beethoven__

c) Add the Time Signature directly on the music.

d) How many counts does the rest at the letter **A** receive? __1__

e) Name the notes at the letters **B**: __B__   **C**: __D__

f) Name the interval at **D** (number size only). __4__

g) Circle the name of the rest at the letter **E**.   (Eighth)   Quarter   Half

h) Find a Tonic triad of G Major in this excerpt and circle it. Label it G Maj.

i) How many times does the note F# appear in this excerpt? __one__

j) How many slurs are in this excerpt? __three__

UltimateMusicTheory.com © Copyright 2013 Gloryland Publishing. All Rights Reserved.

ULTIMATE MUSIC THEORY
PREPARATORY EXAM SET #2 - EXAM #2

Total Score: ___ / 100

1. a) Name the following notes.
   b) Draw a line from each note to the corresponding key on the keyboard (at the correct pitch).

___ / 10

G   C   E   D   A   G

c) Write the following notes in the Treble Clef. Use half notes.

A   C#   C♮   D♭

ULTIMATE MUSIC THEORY
PREPARATORY EXAM SET #2 - EXAM #2

2. a) For each pair of notes, circle the note which sounds lower in pitch. Name the notes.

b) Indicate whether the distance between the notes in each measure is a semitone (half step) or a whole tone (whole step) by circling either SEMITONE or WHOLE TONE.

ULTIMATE MUSIC THEORY
PREPARATORY EXAM SET #2 - EXAM #2

3. a) Name each of the following melodic intervals. (Write the number size only.)

b) Write a note above each of the given notes to form the following harmonic intervals. Use whole notes.

4. Add rests below each bracket to complete each measure.

ULTIMATE MUSIC THEORY
PREPARATORY EXAM SET #2 - EXAM #2

5. a) Identify the following scales as C major, F Major or G Major.
   b) In each scale, circle one Tonic note. Label it as I.

10

Scale: C Major

Scale: G Major

Scale: F Major

Scale: G Major

Scale: C Major

ULTIMATE MUSIC THEORY
PREPARATORY EXAM SET #2 - EXAM #2

6. Match each triad name with the correct triad.

$\overline{10}$ G Major Triad, Broken, in the Treble Clef   __e__   a)

F Major Triad, Solid, in the Treble Clef   __c__   b)

C Major Triad, Solid, in the Bass Clef   __d__   c)

C Major Triad, Broken, in the Treble Clef   __a__   d)

G Major Triad, Solid, in the Bass Clef   __b__   e)

UltimateMusicTheory.com © Copyright 2013 Gloryland Publishing. All Rights Reserved.

ULTIMATE MUSIC THEORY
PREPARATORY EXAM SET #2 - EXAM #2

7. a) Name each of the following rests. Do not use abbreviations.

10

▬ = whole rest

▬ = half rest

𝄽 = quarter rest

𝄾 = eighth rest

b) Draw an example of each of the following notes. Observe the stem direction.

a quarter note (stem pointing down) =

a single eighth note (stem pointing up) =

a dotted half note (stem pointing down) =

a single eighth note (stem pointing down) =

a dotted quarter note (stem pointing up) =

two eighth notes joined with a beam (stems pointing down) =

ULTIMATE MUSIC THEORY
PREPARATORY EXAM SET #2 - EXAM #2

8. a) Add bar lines to complete the following rhythms.

b) Add the correct Time Signature below each bracket.

ULTIMATE MUSIC THEORY
PREPARATORY EXAM SET #2 - EXAM #2

9. Write the correct Italian term for the following definitions. Do not use signs or abbreviations.

___ / 10

Definition	Italian Term
soft	piano
at a moderate tempo	moderato
becoming louder	crescendo
detached	staccato
medium loud	mezzo forte
smooth	legato
very slow	largo
slowing down gradually	ritardando
return to the original tempo	a tempo
moderately slow; at a walking pace	andante

UltimateMusicTheory.com © Copyright 2013 Gloryland Publishing. All Rights Reserved.

ULTIMATE MUSIC THEORY
PREPARATORY EXAM SET #2 - EXAM #2

10. Analyze the following piece of music by answering the questions below.

a) Name the title of this piece. __Getting Dizzy!__

b) Explain the tempo of this piece. __Allegro -fast__

c) Add the Time Signature directly on the music.

e) Add a dynamic sign in measure 1 that indicates to play loud (forte).

d) Name the notes at the letters A: __C__   B: __D__

f) Add dots to the notes in the Bass Clef at measure 2 to create staccato quarter notes.

g) Explain the signs at C and D. __Repeat the music within the double bar lines__

h) Add the missing rest in measure 4 at E.

i) Name the rest in measure 4 at F. __eighth rest__

j) Circle one example of a fermata. Label it fermata.

ULTIMATE MUSIC THEORY
PREPARATORY EXAM SET #2 - EXAM #3

Total Score: ___ / 100

1. a) Write the notes on the Grand Staff for the keys marked with a ☺. Use whole notes.
   b) Name the notes.
   c) Draw a line from each note to the corresponding key on the keyboard (at the correct pitch).

___/10

B   F   E   D

d) Name the following notes.

B♭   C   E♯   D   A♯   A

UltimateMusicTheory.com © Copyright 2013 Gloryland Publishing. All Rights Reserved.

ULTIMATE MUSIC THEORY
PREPARATORY EXAM SET #2 - EXAM #3

2. a) For each pair of notes, circle the note which sounds higher in pitch. Name the notes.

10

b) Beside each note, write the note that is one whole tone (whole step) lower. Use whole notes. Name the notes.

ULTIMATE MUSIC THEORY
PREPARATORY EXAM SET #2 - EXAM #3

3. a) Name the interval at each of the following letters. (Write the number size only.)

A __3__

B __2__

C __8__

D __3__

E __5__

b) Write a note above each of the given notes to form the following harmonic intervals. Use whole notes.

ULTIMATE MUSIC THEORY
PREPARATORY EXAM SET #2 - EXAM #3

4. Indicate if the rests in each measure are correct or incorrect by circling either CORRECT or INCORRECT.

ULTIMATE MUSIC THEORY
PREPARATORY EXAM SET #2 - EXAM #3

5.   a) Write the scale of F Major, descending (going down) one octave. Use accidentals instead of a Key Signature. Use whole notes. Circle one Tonic note. Label it as I.

   b) Write the scale of G Major, ascending (going up) one octave. Use accidentals instead of a Key Signature. Use whole notes. Circle one Tonic note. Label it as I.

   c) Write the scale of F Major, ascending (going up) one octave. Use a Key Signature. Use whole notes. Circle one Tonic note. Label it as I.

   d) Write the scale of C Major, descending (going down) one octave. Use a Key Signature. Use whole notes. Circle one Tonic note. Label it as I.

ULTIMATE MUSIC THEORY
PREPARATORY EXAM SET #2 - EXAM #3

6. Write the following solid (blocked) triads in Root Position on the Tonic note. Use whole notes.

___
10

F Major triad in the Bass Clef.
Use accidentals.

C Major triad in the Treble Clef.
Use a Key Signature.

G Major triad in the Bass Clef.
Use a Key Signature.

F Major triad in the Treble Clef.
Use a Key Signature.

C Major triad in the Bass Clef.
Use accidentals.

ULTIMATE MUSIC THEORY
PREPARATORY EXAM SET #2 - EXAM #3

7. a) Draw the following rests.

    ___/10

    quarter rest = 𝄽

    half rest = ▬

    eighth rest = 𝄾

    whole rest = ▬

b) Write the number of counts received when the notes are added together.

example: ♪ ♪ ♪	=	1½
𝅗𝅥 ♩	=	3
𝅗𝅥. ♪	=	2
♫	=	1
𝅗𝅥. ♩	=	4
♪ ♪	=	1
♪ ♪ ♩	=	2

ULTIMATE MUSIC THEORY
PREPARATORY EXAM SET #2 - EXAM #3

8. a) Add bar lines to complete the following rhythms.

b) Add the correct Time Signature below each bracket.

ULTIMATE MUSIC THEORY
PREPARATORY EXAM SET #2 - EXAM #3

9. Circle the correct term for each of the following signs or symbols.

__10__

Sign or Symbol	Term		
f	piano	or	(forte)
mp	(mezzo piano)	or	mezzo forte
$<$	(crescendo)	or	decrescendo
♩‿♩♩	tie	or	(slur)
mf	mezzo piano	or	(mezzo forte)
♩·	legato	or	(staccato)
$>$	crescendo	or	(diminuendo)
♩‿♩	(tie)	or	slur
♭	sharp	or	(flat)
𝄐	(fermata)	or	natural

UltimateMusicTheory.com © Copyright 2013 Gloryland Publishing. All Rights Reserved.

ULTIMATE MUSIC THEORY
PREPARATORY EXAM SET #2 - EXAM #3

10. Analyze the following excerpt of music by answering the questions below.

Minuet in F Major

Allegro G. F. Handel

a) Name the title of this excerpt. **Minuet in F Major**

b) Explain the tempo of this excerpt. **Allegro - fast**

c) Name the composer of this excerpt. **G. F. Handel**

e) Add the Time Signature directly on the music.

d) Explain the dynamic sign in measure 1. **mezzo forte - moderately loud**

f) Name the notes at the letters   A: **D**   B: **B♭**

g) Explain the dynamic sign in measure 2. **crescendo - becoming louder**

h) Name the interval (number size only) at   C: **5**   D: **2**

i) Name the interval (number size only) at   E: **8**   F: **1**

j) How many times does the note B♭ appear in this excerpt? **three**

UltimateMusicTheory.com © Copyright 2013 Gloryland Publishing. All Rights Reserved.

ULTIMATE MUSIC THEORY
PREPARATORY EXAM SET #2 - EXAM #4

Total Score: ___ / 100

1. a) Name the following notes.
   b) Draw a line from each note to the corresponding key on the keyboard (at the correct pitch).

___/10

A   D   A   F   C   F

c) Write the following notes in the Treble Clef. Use dotted half notes.

G   F#   F♮   F♭

ULTIMATE MUSIC THEORY
PREPARATORY EXAM SET #2 - EXAM #4

2. a) For each pair of notes, circle the note which sounds higher in pitch. Name the notes.

b) Indicate whether the distance between the notes in each measure is a semitone (half step) or a whole tone (whole step) by circling either SEMITONE or WHOLE TONE.

ULTIMATE MUSIC THEORY
PREPARATORY EXAM SET #2 - EXAM #4

3. a) Name each of the following harmonic intervals. (Write the number size only.)

b) Write a note above each of the given notes to form the following melodic intervals. Use half notes.

4. Add rests below each bracket to complete each measure.

ULTIMATE MUSIC THEORY
PREPARATORY EXAM SET #2 - EXAM #4

5. a) Write the scale of G Major, descending (going down) one octave. Use accidentals instead of a Key Signature. Use whole notes. Circle one Tonic note. Label it as **I**.

b) Write the scale of F Major, ascending (going up) one octave. Use accidentals instead of a Key Signature. Use whole notes. Circle one Tonic note. Label it as **I**.

c) Write the scale of C Major, ascending (going up) one octave. Use a Key Signature. Use whole notes. Circle one Tonic note. Label it as **I**.

d) Write the scale of F Major, descending (going down) one octave. Use a Key Signature. Use whole notes. Circle one Tonic note. Label it as **I**.

ULTIMATE MUSIC THEORY
PREPARATORY EXAM SET #2 - EXAM #4

6. Match each triad name with the correct triad.

__10__

G Major Triad, Broken, in the Bass Clef _c_

a)

G Major Triad, Solid, in the Treble Clef _e_

b)

F Major Triad, Solid, in the Bass Clef _a_

c)

C Major Triad, Broken, in the Treble Clef _b_

d)

C Major Triad, Solid, in the Bass Clef _d_

e)

UltimateMusicTheory.com © Copyright 2013 Gloryland Publishing. All Rights Reserved.

ULTIMATE MUSIC THEORY
PREPARATORY EXAM SET #2 - EXAM #4

7. a) Name the following rests. Do not use abbreviations.

   10

   ▬ = whole rest

   𝄽 = quarter rest

   𝄾 = eighth rest

   ▬ = half rest

   b) Write the number of counts received when the rests are added together.

   example: ▬ 𝄾 𝄾 = 3

   𝄾 𝄾 = 1

   𝄽 𝄾 = 1½

   𝄽 𝄽 𝄽 𝄽 = 4

   𝄽 ▬ = 3

   ▬ ▬ = 4

   ▬ 𝄽 𝄽 = 4

ULTIMATE MUSIC THEORY
PREPARATORY EXAM SET #2 - EXAM #4

8. a) Add bar lines to complete the following rhythms.

b) Add the correct Time Signature below each bracket.

ULTIMATE MUSIC THEORY
PREPARATORY EXAM SET #2 - EXAM #4

9. Circle the correct definition for each of the following terms.

___
10

Term	Definition		
legato	**(smooth)**	or	slow
mezzo forte	moderately soft	or	**(moderately loud)**
crescendo	**(becoming louder)**	or	becoming softer
ritardando	**(slowing down gradually)**	or	becoming faster
largo	very smooth	or	**(very slow)**
moderato	fast	or	**(at a moderate tempo)**
decrescendo	becoming louder	or	**(becoming softer)**
piano	**(soft)**	or	loud
slur	**(play the notes legato)**	or	a unit of musical time
fermata	detached	or	**(hold the note or rest longer than the written value)**

ULTIMATE MUSIC THEORY
PREPARATORY EXAM SET #2 - EXAM #4

10. Analyze the following excerpt of music by answering the questions below.

Minuet in G Major

Moderato   G. F. Handel

a) Name the title of this excerpt. __Minuet in G Major__

b) Explain the tempo of this excerpt. __Moderato - at a Moderate tempo__

c) Add the Time Signature directly on the music.

e) Name the Key of this excerpt. __G Major__

d) Explain the dynamic sign in measure 1. __mezzo piano - Moderately soft__

f) Name the notes at the letters **A**: __A__   **B**: __D__

g) Is the curved line in measure 2 a tie or a slur? __slur__

h) Name the intervals at the letters **C**: __2__   **D**: __1__

i) How many times does the note F# appear in this excerpt? __three__

j) What is the highest note in this piece? __E__

UltimateMusicTheory.com © Copyright 2013 Gloryland Publishing. All Rights Reserved.

ULTIMATE MUSIC THEORY EXAM SERIES

_____   _____

UltimateMusicTheory.com © Copyright 2013 Gloryland Publishing. All Rights Reserved.

ULTIMATE MUSIC THEORY EXAM SERIES

UltimateMusicTheory.com © Copyright 2013 Gloryland Publishing. All Rights Reserved.

ULTIMATE MUSIC THEORY EXAM SERIES

UltimateMusicTheory.com © Copyright 2013 Gloryland Publishing. All Rights Reserved.

Ultimate Music Theory

Workbooks, Exams, Answers, Online Courses, App & More!

A Proven Step-by-Step System to Learn Theory Faster - from Beginner to Advanced.

Innovative techniques designed to develop a complete understanding of music theory, to enhance sight reading, ear training, creativity, composition and musical expression.

All UMT Series have matching Answer Books!

The UMT Rudiments Series - Beginner A, Beginner B, Beginner C, Prep 1, Prep 2, Basic, Intermediate, Advanced & Complete (All-In-One)

- ♪ 12 Lessons, Review Tests, and a Final Exam to develop confidence
- ♪ Music Theory Guide & Chart for fast and easy reference of theory concepts
- ♪ 80 Flashcards for fun drills to dramatically increase retention & comprehension

Rudiments Exam Series - Preparatory, Basic, Intermediate & Advanced

- ♪ 8 Exams plus UMT Tips on How to Score 100% on Theory Exams

Each Rudiments Workbook correlates to a Supplemental Workbook.

The UMT Supplemental Series - Prep Level, Level 1, Level 2, Level 3, Level 4, Level 5, Level 6, Level 7, Level 8 & Complete (All-In-One) Level

- ♪ Form & Analysis and Music History - Composers, Eras & Musical Styles
- ♪ Melody Writing using ICE - Imagine, Compose & Explore
- ♪ 12 Lessons, Review Tests, Final Exam and 80 Flashcards for quick study

Supplemental Exam Series - Level 5, Level 6, Level 7 & Level 8

- ♪ 8 Exams to successfully prepare for nationally recognized Theory Exams

UMT Online Courses, Music Theory App & More

- ♪ UMT Certification Course, Teachers Membership & Elite Educator Program
- ♪ Ultimate Music Theory App correlates to the Rudiments Workbooks
- ♪ Free Resources - Teachers Guide, Music Theory Blogs, videos & downloads

Go To: **UltimateMusicTheory.com**